KISS
Sing
PROMISE
NAME
BLESS
Greet
Touch
HONOR
ANNOUNCE
Hold
Celebrate
Play
TREASURE
GIVE GIFTS

KISS
Sing
NAME
BLESS
PROMISE
HONOR
Touch
Greet
ANNOUNCE
Hold
Celebrate
Play
TREASURE
GIVE GIFTS

WELCOMING
BABIES

MARGY BURNS KNIGHT

Illustrated by ANNE SIBLEY O'BRIEN

TILBURY HOUSE PUBLISHERS, THOMASTON, MAINE

In memory of Marcia Seward Knight,
Emilie and Kyle's grandma.
—MBK

For two of the babies in my life: my goddaughter
Elizabeth Virginia Hart, long awaited; and in
memory of Oliver Pentland Huber.
—ASOB

A Note from Margy

The inspiration for *Welcoming Babies* came from my daughter Emilie. When she was five years old, during her grandmother's memorial service, Emilie asked me, "Mom, do they do things like this when babies are born?"

"Yes, Emilie," I whispered, "there are many ways to say hello to babies."

Later I shared Emilie's question with Anne Sibley O'Brien, and *Welcoming Babies* was born. Since the first edition was published all those years ago, many of the babies featured in these stories, including our own children, have grown up to have babies of their own. Annie's daughter Yunhee welcomed a son Taemin in 2014, and the next year the family celebrated his first birthday Korean-style. In 2017 Emilie welcomed a daughter, Penney Florence, who wore her great-grandfather's hundred-year-old christening gown at a welcoming party in her parents' backyard.

While sharing *Welcoming Babies* over the years, I have been introduced to many additional welcoming stories. I've included some of my favorites in the back of the book.

—MBK

Every day, everywhere, babies are born.
We have many ways to show them we are
glad they came into the world.

We Sing

Afam is a brand-new baby. When the women near his house hear his first cry, they begin to sing, "Beautiful one, beautiful one, welcome!" When other women hear the song, they join in. Soon Afam's whole village will know that a new baby has been born.

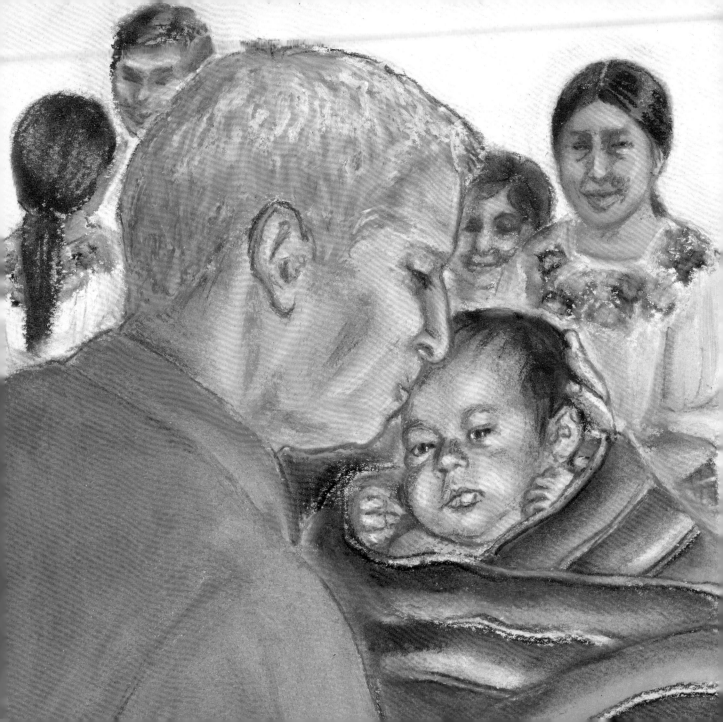

We Kiss

Maria and Tomas are eight days old. Today the door of their home is opened for visitors who greet the twins with kisses. Candles are lit, and a special meal is served to celebrate the birth of the babies.

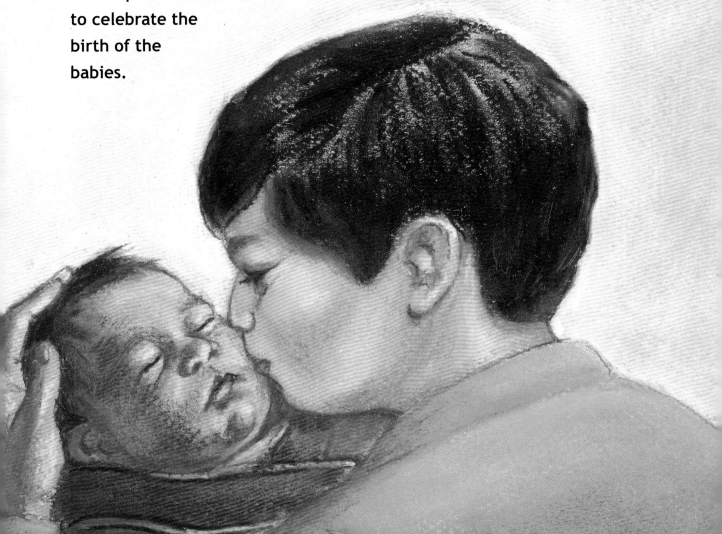

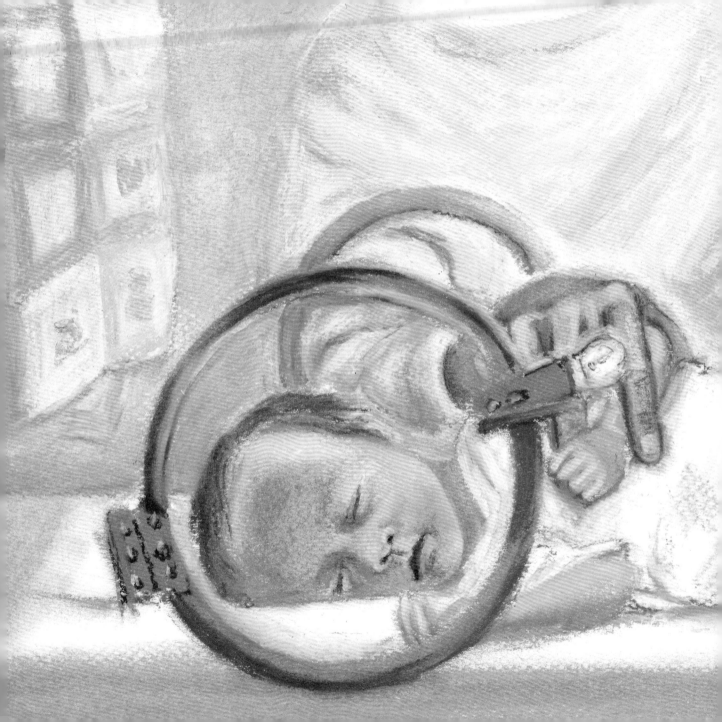

We Touch

Many times every day Luke's parents gently rub him. His
cousins have sent him a musical doll so he can
listen to "My Favorite Things" in his incubator.
Nurses and doctors will take good care of
Luke until he is ready to go home.

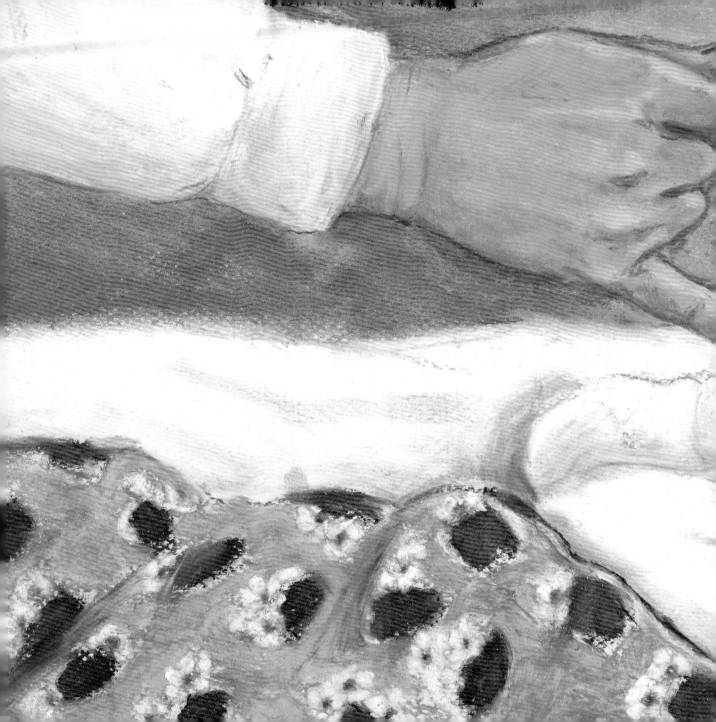

We Bless

A tiny drop of sugar butter is placed on Cyrus's tongue by the midwife so that he will have a sweet life. Soon his grandfather will whisper prayers to Allah into each of Cyrus's ears.

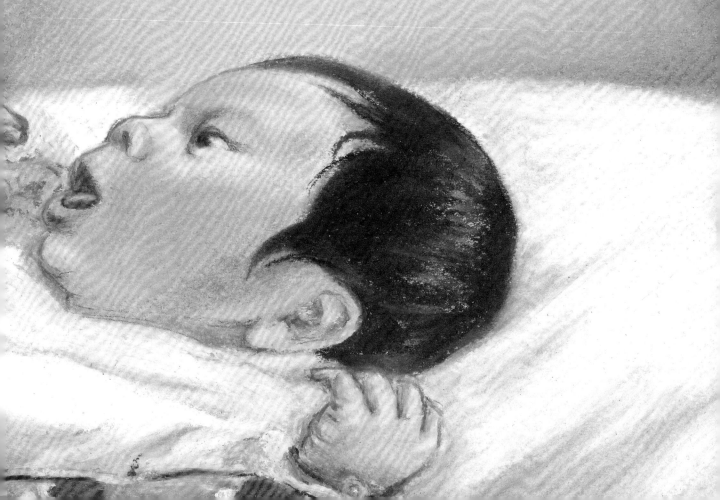

We Name

Jeff and Judi say Hebrew prayers for their infant daughter Rachel, whom they named for Jeff's mother. Rabbi Ascher and the congregation join them in prayer during Rachel's naming ceremony.

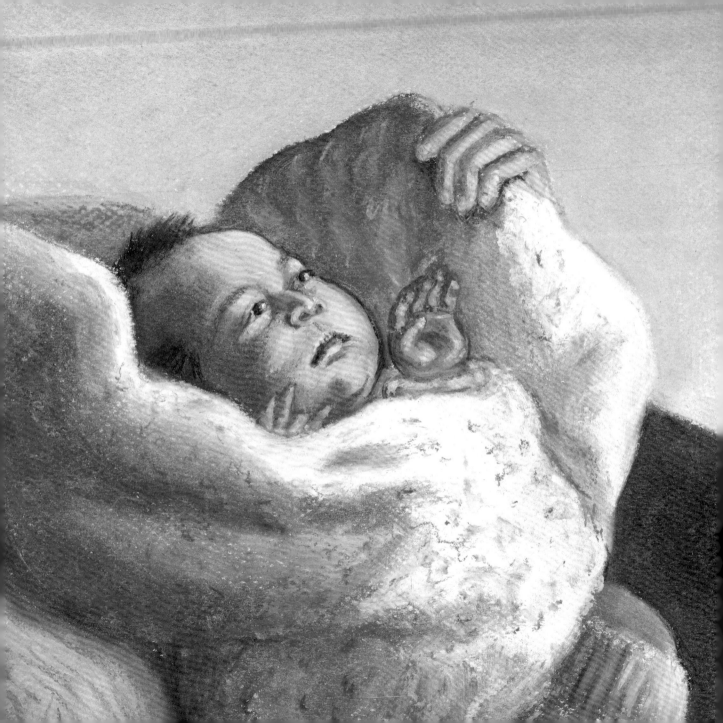

We Greet

Kasa was born twenty days ago, and today is her naming ceremony. Her grandmother, who chose her name, lifts the blanket off Kasa's tiny face. She holds her granddaughter up to greet the first rays of the early morning sun.

We Promise

Reverend Lawson places a drop of water on Alexis's forehead. Her parents promise to teach her about god as she grows. With this baptism, Alexis is welcomed into the Christian church.

We Announce

Lidia and Jason want to tell their friends and family how excited
they are about their new sister. The cards
they send have two special dates:
the day Rosa was born and the
day she came into their
family by adoption.

Tom, Alice, Jason & Lidia
are happy to announ
the arrival of
Rosa Helena

Born April 16, 1994
São Paulo, Brazil
Came home
August 4, 1994

We Hold

Joseph's friends and relatives sit in a circle during Sunday meeting. Each person holds baby Joseph to greet him. Emilie waits for her turn to hold Joseph. She wants to hold him all by herself.

We Celebrate

Carmen loves her new cousin Ricardo. At the christening
party given by his godparents, she and the other guests
wear *encintados*. These colorful ribbons show the names
of Ricardo and his godparents.

We Give Gifts

Lia's *yai-yai* shows her granddaughter the presents she placed under Lia's pillow the day she was born. A sprinkle of sugar, a few grains of rice, and a silver coin are meant to give Lia a sweet, sturdy, rich life. Yai-yai placed these in a small piece of cotton so that Lia might live long enough to have white hair.

We Honor

In the springtime following her birth, Baby Anna's family plants her celebration tree. Each year on her September birthday, the leaves of this maple will be bright red.

We Play

Darrell and his father love to play together.
Each morning as they get ready for their day,
they play the same special games. Darrell
always makes his father laugh.

We Treasure

For her first birthday, Ok-hee's family fills the table with gifts and food. Those who treasure her gather to wish Ok-hee a long and happy life.

We share the same wish for babies everywhere.

More Welcoming Babies

Sing

Afam is an Igboo baby born in Nigeria. In many villages throughout Africa, babies are welcomed with songs.

In parts of **Morocco**, a communal cry of joy is sung by women to announce to the neighborhood that a birth has occurred.

In the **United States**, Navajos chant a special song at important times in a person's life. "The Blessing Way" is sung as a baby is about to be born. It is thought to ensure health, harmony, and prosperity.

Kiss

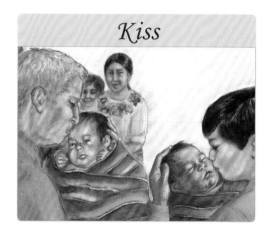

Maria and Tomas are Quiché twins who live in Guatemala. For the first eight days of life, Quiché babies stay with their mothers, and friends bring food and gifts. On the eighth day the babies are bathed and dressed in new clothes. After the house is cleaned and candles are lit, the doors are opened so that neighbors and relatives can kiss the babies and have a big feast.

Touch

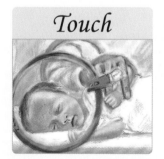

All babies are touched. Babies who must stay in incubators after they are born may be touched only through holes in the side of the incubator. The parents long for the day they can hold their baby in their arms.

Massage is a loving touch that many babies all over the world enjoy. In many parts of **India**, one- to six-month-old babies are massaged regularly by their mothers with coconut or diluted mustard oil. This tradition is often passed down from mother to daughter.

In the **Philippines**, a traditionally trained *hilot* massages babies and their mothers.

Bless

Cyrus's parents were born in Afghanistan and are Muslims. In some Afghani families, babies are fed sugar butter for the first six days. The sugar butter also symbolizes cleansing.

In parts of **Pakistan**, an elder feeds a new baby *gutki* by putting a fingertip of molasses in the baby's mouth.

In **Senegal**, Muslims write prayers from the Koran on a piece of paper. After they soak the paper in water, they tear off a tiny piece and place it on the newborn's tongue. Seven days after birth, the child's name is whispered three times into each ear.

For generations **Chippewa**, **Lakota**, and **Navajo** grandparents have made and hung a tiny dream catcher by the cradleboard to wish their grandchildren very sweet dreams.

Rachel's ceremony is called *Simchat Bat*, which means "joy of daughter." Her younger brother, Aaron Samuel, had a bris, or *Brit Malah*, which means "covenant of circumcision." Traditionally Jewish children are named after a deceased relative.

Name

In **Tibet**, many babies are given a secret name by a lama, a high priest in the Buddhist faith. The name is written down and worn in a pouch around the neck for life. Babies are given other names to be used by family and friends.

In some **Vietnamese** families, fathers name the sons, and mothers name the daughters.

A naming or "outdooring" ceremony in **Ghana** takes place on the morning of the eighth day after birth. A libation is poured on the ground as a form of prayer asking God to bless the child and his or her ancestors, then the child is named. Songs of praise and advice are sung as the baby is welcomed into the community.

Greet

Kasa's paternal grandmother gave her a Hopi name. She is a member of the Hopi tribe in the United States. On her twentieth day, Kasa's father watches for the sunrise as a group of women walks with her to greet the sun. Kasa's grandmother says a prayer as she takes the blanket away from her granddaughter's face.

At forty days old, a **Greek** baby is greeted in the back of the church by a priest. The priest says a few prayers and carries the baby down the aisle to the altar for the Forty Day or Churching ceremony. The baby will return to church at five months for a baptism ceremony.

Promise

Many Christian communities use baptism to welcome babies into their faith. The water used during the baptism symbolizes life and cleansing.

After baptism in the **Philippines**, when many babies are christened, godparents run to the door of the church holding their godchild. The first child out of the church may grow up to be a leader.

Announce

Lidia and Jason announced their adopted sister's arrival with a homemade card.

Some families make phone calls or put a notice in the newspaper to announce the coming of a new baby.

In ancient **Rome**, an olive branch for a boy or a strip of woolen fabric for a girl was hung from the front door to announce the baby's arrival.

Cambodian mothers tie a string of tiny bells around their infants' ankles. A sign of good luck, the gentle ringing of the bells reminds everyone that a new baby has arrived. After the bells are removed, they are put in a safe place and kept as a family memento.

Hold

Joseph is being welcomed to his Quaker Meeting.

In Zaire, many **Mbuti** people welcome babies by standing in a circle and passing the child among them so the baby can be held and greeted by members of the community.

In some **Iranian** families, new babies are passed around a circle and each person whispers prayers to Allah into the infant's ears.

Dressed in a new outfit, an **Egyptian** baby is carried around the house during *Sebou*, the seventh-day ceremony. Guests and family follow the procession with candles. After a meal, visitors are given candy and silver and gold coins.

Throughout Spanish-speaking Latin America, parties are given by the *compadre* and *comadre*, the godparents, for their godchildren after they are baptized.

In many **Puerto Rican** communities, after a feast of roast pig, pigeon peas, and salad, each guest takes home an *encintado*.

Chinese parents throw a one-month party for their infant. Guests bring money in lucky red envelopes, because red is a symbol of happiness and new life. The baby's family gives red eggs to their guests to celebrate their baby.

Once a year the district of Lilley, **Australia**, hosts a Welcoming the Babies Ceremony to recognize the important role parents, grandparents, and guardians play in raising the newest members of the community. At the party, families play games and listen to music, and the babies receive a certificate of welcome to their community.

Celebrate

Give Gifts

Lia's Greek grandma puts cotton, sugar, rice, and coins in a bag for Lia and keeps it in a special place.

Protective amulets are given to babies in **Afghanistan** and the **Philippines**.

In **Cambodia**, strings with money attached to them are tied around babies' wrists.

On the third or fourth day after birth, **Tibetan** family and friends give their new baby a *kata*, or blessing scarf. The ceremonial white cloth is gently wrapped around the baby to welcome him or her to the family and community. Visitors bring small presents and share butter tea and cookies.

Anna lives in Maine, and her tree was chosen because of her September birthday. Her brother Nathan's birch tree was planted because Nathan was named after his grandfather, who loved birch trees. Little sister Kimberly's tree is an evergreen because she was born in December.

In the **Jewish** ceremony a tree is planted at the birth of a child: a cedar for a boy and a pine for a girl. When a couple marries, their birth trees are cut down and used to build a *huppah*, or wedding pavilion.

In **Switzerland**, an apple tree is often planted for the birth of a boy and a nut tree for a girl.

In the **Philippines**, a tree is often planted where the umbilical cord was buried.

Honor

Play

All over the world, people play peek-a-boo with babies. They also play clapping, bouncing, finger, and toe games. Many families have special baby games that they pass down from generation to generation.

Treasure

Ok-hee is Korean. First and sixtieth birthdays are the only two birthdays celebrated in Korea. In all other years, people count themselves a year older on Lunar New Year. The objects on Ok-hee's birthday table are symbols for her future: yarn for a long life, money for wealth, a notebook so she will grow up to be a good student. Rice cakes, candy, and fruit are also on the table.

Tilbury House Publishers
12 Starr Street
Thomaston, Maine 04861
800-582-1899 • www.tilburyhouse.com

Text © 1994, 2018 by Margy Burns Knight • Illustrations © 1994, 2018 by Anne Sibley O'Brien

Hardcover ISBN 978-088448-641-1 • eBook ISBN 978-9-88448-642-8

First hardcover printing March 2018

15 16 17 18 19 20 XXX 10 9 8 7 6 5 4 3 2 1

Printed in China

Library of Congress Control Number: 2018900209

Cover and interior designed by Frame25 Productions

A special thanks to the following: Jay Hoffman and the University of Maine at Augusta Library, Donna Headrick, Christi and Ricardo Moraga, the Bender family, the Toothaker family, Ifi Amadiume, Reverend Margaret Lawson, Bill Myer, the Claman-Kaledin family, Ali Kahn, Gladys and Burtt Richardson, the Habibzai family, the McIlwain family, Steve Downe, Dianne Webb, Pam Osborn, Nancy McGinnis, Sue Cannon, Teri Grant, Debbie Mihalakies, Steve Notis, Mary Haeri, and Chun Taylor.

MARGY BURNS KNIGHT received the National Education Association's Author-Illustrator Human & Civil Rights Award for her work with Anne Sibley O'Brien and the Children's Africana Book Award for *Africa Is Not a Country*. She is the author of *Talking Walls* and *Welcoming Babies*; writes the blog "Discover Your World"; and is a Service Learning Coordinator, an English teacher, and a Peace Corps veteran.

ANNE SIBLEY O'BRIEN has illustrated 31 books, including *Talking Walls* and *Welcoming Babies*, and is the author and illustrator of the picture book *I'm New Here* and the graphic novel *The Legend of Hong Kil Dong*. Annie's passion for multicultural subjects grew out of her experience of being raised in South Korea as the daughter of medical missionaries. She writes the column "The Illustrator's Perspective" for the *Bulletin of the Society of Children's Book Writers and Illustrators* and the blog "Coloring Between the Lines."

KISS
Sing
NAME
BLESS
PROMISE
HONOR
Touch
Greet
ANNOUNCE
Hold
Play
Celebrate
GIVE GIFTS
TREASURE

GIVE GIFTS PROMISE Play Celebrate TREASURE Sing
KISS HONOR
ANNOUNCE Touch NAME Celebrate
Hold Sing Touch GIVE GIFTS
Greet BLESS KISS TREASURE
KISS Celebrate HONOR
Touch Greet NAME BLESS Touch
ANNOUNCE Greet Touch PROMISE ANNOUNCE KISS
Touch Sing BLESS NAME
ANNOUNCE Greet PROMISE Sing KISS Celebrate
PROMISE Celebrate PROMISE BLESS GIVE GIFTS Greet
HONOR TREASURE PROMISE Celebrate
NAME Sing PROMISE Play Play Hold
Sing PROMISE ANNOUNCE HONOR Play BLESS
HONOR BLESS Greet Sing
NAME Sing Hold ANNOUNCE Greet Hold Hold Touch
BLESS ANNOUNCE HONOR Greet BLESS
Sing Greet TREASURE
Hold Play KISS TREASURE
Touch Hold NAME GIVE GIFTS GIVE GIFTS Touch Play HONOR Greet KISS
BLESS Hold PROMISE Celebrate GIVE GIFTS Celebrate HONOR Play
NAME Celebrate HONOR Play
ANNOUNCE ANNOUNCE HONOR TREASURE Touch HONOR
Sing Play Celebrate KISS Hold Greet
BLESS Play Celebrate Play HONOR NAME HONOR
NAME KISS HONOR Hold
Sing PROMISE BLESS Greet TREASURE
KISS Sing Greet Play Play
BLESS Play Hold